United States Presidents

James Buchanan

Paul Joseph
ABDO Publishing Company

visit us at
www.abdopub.com

Published by ABDO Publishing Company 4940 Viking Drive, Edina, Minnesota 55435. Copyright © 2000 by Abdo Consulting Group, Inc. International copyrights reserved in all countries. No part of this book may be reproduced in any form without written permission from the publisher.

Published 2000
Printed in the United States of America
Second Printing 2002

Photo credits: Archive Photos, UPI/Corbis-Bettmann

Contributing editors: Bob Italia, Tamara L. Britton, K. M. Brielmaier, Kate A. Furlong

Library of Congress Cataloging-in-Publication Data

Joseph, Paul, 1970-
    James Buchanan / Paul Joseph.
        p. cm. -- (United States presidents)
    Includes index.
    Summary: A biography of the man who served as the fifteenth president of the United States just before the Civil War.
    ISBN 1-57765-241-X
    1. Buchanan, James, 1791-1868--Juvenile literature.
2. Presidents--United States--Biography--Juvenile literature. [1. Buchanan, James, 1791-1868. 2. Presidents.] I. Title. II. Series: United States presidents (Edina, Minn.)
E437.J68 1999
973.6'8'092--dc21
    [B]   98-19317
                                                                              CIP
                                                                               AC

Contents

James Buchanan

*J*ames Buchanan became the fifteenth U.S. president in 1857. He was 65 years old. He had worked in politics for 33 years.

Buchanan's career was respected and distinguished. He was a United States congressman and senator. He was minister to Russia and Great Britain. He was also **secretary of state**.

Buchanan became president during a difficult time in the nation's history. The Northern and Southern states were arguing over slavery. The country was about to come apart.

Buchanan hoped he could keep the country united. But the slavery problem was too difficult to fix. The South **seceded** from the Union, leading to the **Civil War**.

James Buchanan

James Buchanan (1791-1868)
Fifteenth President

BORN:	April 23, 1791
PLACE OF BIRTH:	Near Mercersburg, Pennsylvania
ANCESTRY:	Scots-Irish
FATHER:	James Buchanan (1761-1821)
MOTHER:	Elizabeth Speer Buchanan (1767-1833)
WIFE:	Never married
CHILDREN:	None
EDUCATION:	Old Stone Academy, Dickinson College
RELIGION:	Presbyterian
OCCUPATION:	Lawyer, author
MILITARY SERVICE:	Volunteer in special company of Third Cavalry
POLITICAL PARTY:	Democratic

OFFICES HELD:	Member of Pennsylvania legislature, member of U.S. House of Representatives, minister to Russia, U.S. senator, secretary of state, minister to Great Britain
AGE AT INAUGURATION:	65
YEARS SERVED:	1857-1861
VICE PRESIDENT:	John C. Breckinridge
DIED:	June 1, 1868, Lancaster, Pennsylvania, age 77
CAUSE OF DEATH:	Pneumonia and endocarditis

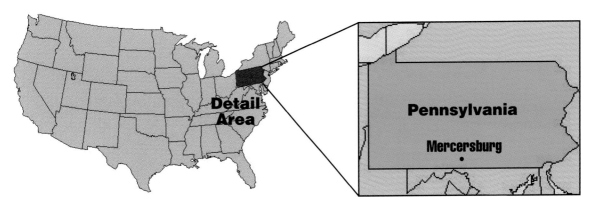

Birthplace of James Buchanan

Young James

*J*ames Buchanan was born near Mercersburg, Pennsylvania, on April 23, 1791. His father, also named James, was a successful storekeeper and landowner. His mother, Elizabeth, taught James to read and enjoy books.

James went to school in Mercersburg. He was a good student who excelled in Latin and Greek.

When he was only 16, James entered Dickinson College. He graduated with honors in 1809. James then studied law in Lancaster. Three years later, he became a lawyer.

Buchanan was a successful lawyer. He was smart and had excellent public speaking skills. But Buchanan wanted to enter politics.

Buchanan's birthplace near Mercersburg, Pennsylvania

Politics and Tragedy

*I*n 1814, Buchanan was elected to the Pennsylvania **legislature**. Buchanan belonged to the **Federalist** party. He served in the legislature for two years.

During this time, Buchanan became engaged to Ann Coleman. Their engagement ended because of a quarrel. Soon after, Ann died. Buchanan was heartbroken. He never married and is the nation's only unmarried president.

In 1820, Buchanan was elected to the United States **House of Representatives**. There, he served as chairman of the House Judiciary Committee. The Judiciary Committee handles civil and criminal judicial matters.

Buchanan was also the **prosecutor** in the **impeachment** trial of James H. Peck. Peck was a

Missouri district court judge. He ruled against the Soulard family, who was trying to claim some public land.

The Soulards' lawyer, Luke Lawless, thought Peck did not follow the law when he made his decision. He spoke out publicly against Peck. Peck imprisoned Lawless and suspended his practice for 18 months. The Senate found Peck innocent.

When the **Federalist** party broke up, Buchanan joined the **Democratic** party. As a Democrat, Buchanan was a strong supporter of President Andrew Jackson.

Buchanan was appointed the minister to Russia in 1831 by President Jackson. As minister, Buchanan arranged the first trade treaty between Russia and the United States.

President Andrew Jackson

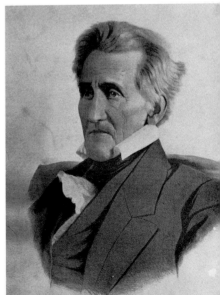

11

Serving His Country

*B*uchanan returned from Russia in 1833. In 1834, he was elected to the U.S. Senate.

Senator Buchanan served as chairman of the Foreign Relations Committee. The Foreign Relations Committee handles the relationships between the U.S. and other countries. He was also chairman of a committee that worked to end the slave trade in Washington, D.C.

Buchanan also helped defeat the "gag rule." The gag rule said no one could talk about slavery in **Congress**. This rule kept laws against slavery from being passed. Congress ended the gag rule in 1844.

Buchanan served in the Senate until 1845. Then he resigned to become the **secretary of state** under President James Polk.

Secretary of State Buchanan believed slavery was legal according to the Constitution. So, he opposed the Wilmot Proviso. The Proviso was an **amendment** proposed by Pennsylvania congressman David Wilmot. The Proviso said that there could be no slavery in territory acquired from Mexico. Buchanan felt that the Proviso was unconstitutional.

But Buchanan knew many Americans did not want slavery. He supported Clay's Compromise, a group of laws proposed by Kentucky senator Henry Clay. Clay's Compromise said that some new states could have slavery and some could not. It also included the Fugitive Slave Act that would return runaway slaves to their owners.

President James Polk

The Making of the Fifteenth United States President

 **1791**
Born April 23 near Mercersburg, Pennsylvania

 **1807**
Enters Dickinson College

 **1809**
Graduates from college

 **1820**
Elected to the U.S. House of Representatives

 1831
Appointed minister to Russia

 **1834**
Elected to U.S. Senate

1856
Elected president

1857
Supreme Court rules on Dred Scott case

1860
Lincoln elected President; Southern states secede

PRESIDENTIAL YEARS

James Buchanan

"Our union rests upon public opinion, and can never be cemented by the blood of its citizens shed in civil war."

 **1812**

Becomes
a lawyer

 **1814**

Elected to the
Pennsylvania
legislature

Historic Events
during Buchanan's Presidency

Pony Express begins mail delivery

First oil well drilled near Titusville,
Pennsylvania

Construction of Suez Canal begins

 **1845**

Appointed secretary
of state under
President Polk

 **1853**

Minister to Great
Britain under
President Pierce

 **1861**

Civil War begins

 **1866**

Publishes
*Mr. Buchanan's
Administration
on the Eve of
the Rebellion*

1868

Dies June 1

Minister to Great Britain

When President Polk's term was over, Buchanan retired as **secretary of state**. He moved to a new house called Wheatland near Lancaster, Pennsylvania.

Because of Buchanan's political experience, many **Democrats** believed he would make a good candidate for president. In 1852, he nearly got the Democratic nomination. Instead, it went to Franklin Pierce.

Buchanan supported Pierce during the presidential election. He gave many speeches on Pierce's behalf. When Pierce won, he made Buchanan the minister to Great Britain.

As minister, Buchanan worked on the Clayton-Bulwer Treaty. This treaty between the U.S. and Great Britain agreed to joint control of any canal or railroad that they might build on the **isthmus** between North and South America.

Buchanan became involved in President Pierce's efforts to acquire Cuba from Spain. He signed the Ostend Manifesto. The Manifesto said that President Pierce should seize Cuba from Spain.

To some Americans, acquiring Cuba was a good idea. It would give the United States more land. But other Americans did not like the idea. Many Northerners believed Cuba would become a Southern state and allow slavery. The government decided against acquiring Cuba.

President Pierce was very unpopular for his Cuba decision. In 1856, he was not renominated by the **Democrats**. Instead, they chose James Buchanan.

President Franklin Pierce

Election of 1856

*I*n the election of 1856, Buchanan faced two opponents. Former president Millard Fillmore ran as the candidate of the American or "Know-Nothing" party. John C. Fremont ran as the candidate of a new party called the **Republicans**.

The Republican party was formed in 1854. It opposed the spread of slavery. Many Northerners, including **Democrats**, joined this new party.

Buchanan received fewer than half of the popular votes. But he won the election because he had the most **electoral** votes. Buchanan received 174 electoral votes, Fremont received 114, and Fillmore received 8.

James Buchanan was **inaugurated** president on March 4, 1857. Buchanan became president as the slavery problem reached its peak. He hoped the problem would be settled in court.

Electoral Votes, 1856

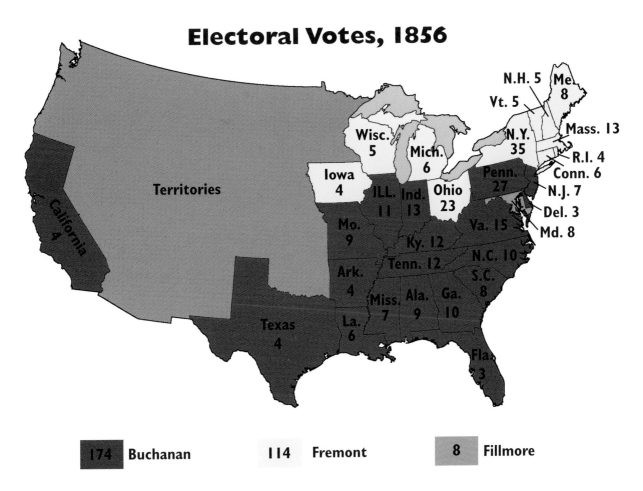

174 Buchanan	**114** Fremont	**8** Fillmore

Each state has electoral votes equal to the number of representatives it has in Congress. The state's population determines its number of representatives. States with large populations get more electoral votes.

When a candidate wins a state's popular vote, he or she wins its electoral votes. Buchanan won enough states to earn the most electoral votes (174). So, he won the 1856 election.

President Buchanan

*I*n 1856, the Supreme Court heard the Dred Scott case. Many hoped this case would settle the slavery problem.

Dred Scott was a Missouri slave who had once lived in Illinois and the Wisconsin Territory. After his owner died, Scott sued for freedom. He said that since he had once lived in both a free state and territory, he was a free man.

In March 1857, the Supreme Court ruled against Scott. Chief Justice Roger Taney stated that slaves were property. The Constitution said that people could not be **deprived** of their property.

President Buchanan supported the Supreme Court's decision. He hoped the slavery problem was settled once and for all. But the Dred Scott decision was hated throughout the North. In the South, Buchanan became known as a defender of slavery.

President Buchanan's troubles continued. In 1855, the Kansas Territory had two governments. There was a proslavery government in Lecompton, and an antislavery government in Topeka. Neither side felt the other was legal. They had bitter battles over slavery. The Territory was called "Bleeding Kansas."

When the Territory adopted a constitution for statehood, the residents had to decide if they wanted slavery or not.

The antislavery people refused to vote because the election was run by the proslavery people. So, even though most people in Kansas were against slavery, a proslavery constitution was passed. It was called the Lecompton Constitution.

Dred Scott

Buchanan supported the Lecompton Constitution. He said he could not override it since it was created by a legal constitutional convention. **Republicans** and Northern **Democrats** were angry. They felt Kansas should be a free state because most of its people were against slavery.

In **Congress**, Senator William English devised the English Bill to **amend** the Lecompton Constitution. This bill would allow Kansas to be a slave state. But it reduced the amount of land Kansas got from the national government. This allowed people in Kansas to vote again on the Lecompton Constitution.

The people of Kansas rejected the Lecompton Constitution. A new constitution was drafted. Kansas entered the Union as a free state in 1861.

On October 16, 1859, **abolitionist** John Brown attempted to seize the U.S. **arsenal** at Harpers Ferry, in present-day West Virginia. He wanted to give the guns to escaped slaves. Brown hoped these slaves would start a revolt in the South.

But national troops arrived October 17. After a fight in which 17 people were killed, John Brown was taken prisoner. He was convicted of treason and hanged on December 2, 1859.

Buchanan had trouble leading a divided nation. Southerners were upset that Kansas was a free state. Northerners were upset that Buchanan defended slavery and supported the judge's decision in the Dred Scott case. It was certain that the **Democrats** would not renominate Buchanan in 1860.

John Brown

The Seven "Hats" of the U.S. President

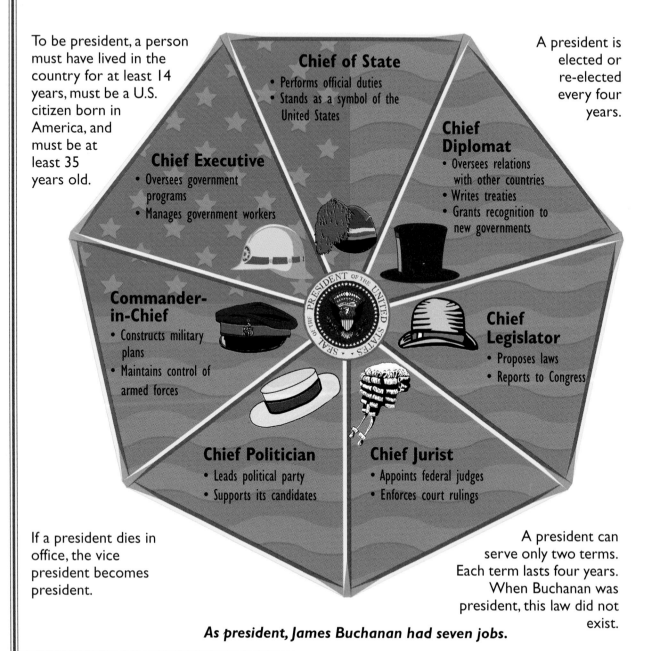

To be president, a person must have lived in the country for at least 14 years, must be a U.S. citizen born in America, and must be at least 35 years old.

A president is elected or re-elected every four years.

Chief of State
- Performs official duties
- Stands as a symbol of the United States

Chief Diplomat
- Oversees relations with other countries
- Writes treaties
- Grants recognition to new governments

Chief Executive
- Oversees government programs
- Manages government workers

Commander-in-Chief
- Constructs military plans
- Maintains control of armed forces

Chief Legislator
- Proposes laws
- Reports to Congress

Chief Politician
- Leads political party
- Supports its candidates

Chief Jurist
- Appoints federal judges
- Enforces court rulings

If a president dies in office, the vice president becomes president.

A president can serve only two terms. Each term lasts four years. When Buchanan was president, this law did not exist.

As president, James Buchanan had seven jobs.

The Three Branches of the U.S. Government

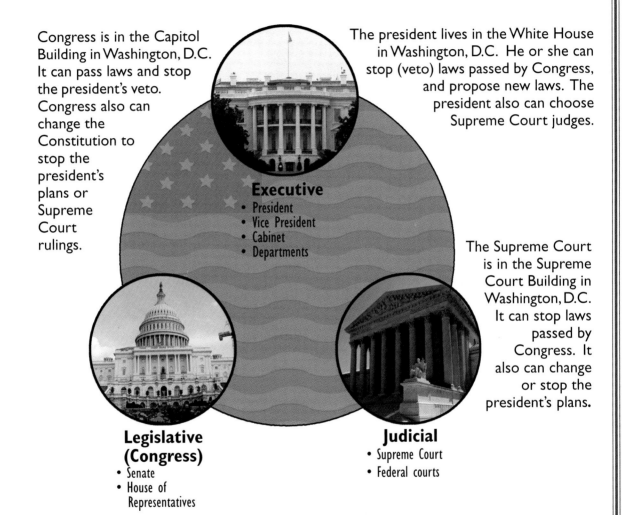

Congress is in the Capitol Building in Washington, D.C. It can pass laws and stop the president's veto. Congress also can change the Constitution to stop the president's plans or Supreme Court rulings.

The president lives in the White House in Washington, D.C. He or she can stop (veto) laws passed by Congress, and propose new laws. The president also can choose Supreme Court judges.

Executive
- President
- Vice President
- Cabinet
- Departments

The Supreme Court is in the Supreme Court Building in Washington, D.C. It can stop laws passed by Congress. It also can change or stop the president's plans.

Legislative (Congress)
- Senate
- House of Representatives

Judicial
- Supreme Court
- Federal courts

The U.S. Constitution formed three government branches. Each branch has power over the others. So, no single group or person can control the country. The Constitution calls this "separation of powers."

After the White House

*I*n 1860, the **Democrats** nominated Illinois senator Stephen A. Douglas for president. But **Republican** candidate Abraham Lincoln won the election.

Buchanan still had another four months in office before Lincoln took over. During that time, seven Southern states—South Carolina, Mississippi, Florida, Alabama, Georgia, Louisiana, and Texas—left the Union and started their own country. They called it the **Confederate States of America**.

On March 4, 1861, Abraham Lincoln arrived at the White House for his **inauguration**. Buchanan told Lincoln that he wished him well in these terrible times. He added that becoming the president was not worth it.

On that bitter note, James Buchanan's long and respected political career came to an end. Buchanan retired to Wheatland. Soon after, the **Civil War** began.

In 1866, Buchanan published a book that defended his actions. He called the book *Mr. Buchanan's* **Administration** *on the Eve of the Rebellion*. Buchanan lived the rest of his life quietly at Wheatland. He died on June 1, 1868.

Abraham Lincoln

Fun Facts

- The first inauguration photographed was Buchanan's in 1857.

- President Buchanan's niece Harriet Lane served as the White House hostess for her unmarried uncle.

- One of Buchanan's eyes was farsighted and one was nearsighted. When he talked he tilted his head to one side to adjust his vision.

- At Wheatland, James Buchanan gave sauerkraut-and-mashed-potato parties.

The United States During Buchanan's Presidency (1857-1861)

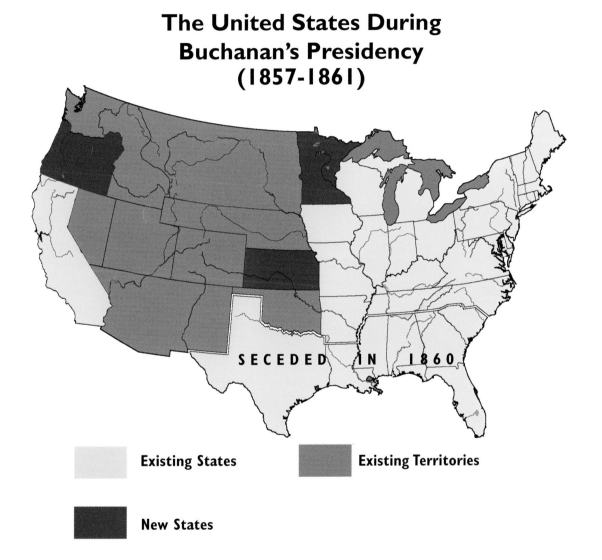

SECEDED IN 1860

Existing States

Existing Territories

New States

Glossary

abolitionist - someone who is against slavery.

administration - the people in charge of running the government.

amendment - a change to a document, such as the Constitution.

arsenal - a collection of weapons, or a place where weapons are made.

Civil War - a war between the Union and the Confederate States of America from 1861 to 1865.

Confederate States of America - the country formed by the eleven southern states that left the Union between 1860 and 1861.

Congress - the lawmaking body of the United States. It is made up of the Senate and the House of Representatives.

Democrat - one of the two main political parties in the United States. Democrats are often more liberal and believe in more government.

deprive - to take something away from someone else.

electoral college - the group that elects the president and vice president by casting electoral votes. When people vote for president, the political party that gets the most votes in each state sends its representatives to the electoral college. There, they vote for their party's candidate.

Federalist - a political party of the U.S. during the early 1800s. Federalists believed in strong national government.

House of Representatives - a group of people elected by citizens to represent them. They meet in Washington, D.C., and make laws for the nation.

impeach - to have a trial to decide if someone should be removed from office.

inaugurate - to be sworn into a political office.

isthmus - a narrow strip of land connecting two larger land areas.

legislature - the lawmaking group of a state or country.

prosecutor - a lawyer who argues to convict the person on trial.

Republican - one of the political parties of the U.S. During the Civil War, Republicans were liberal and against slavery.

secede - to break away from a group.

secretary of state - a member of the president's cabinet who handles problems with other countries.

Internet Sites

United States Presidents Information Page
http://historyoftheworld.com/soquel/prez.htm
Links to information about United States presidents. This site is very informative, with biographies on every president as well as speeches and debates, and other links.

The Presidents of the United States of America
http://www.whitehouse.gov/WH/glimpse/presidents/html/presidents.html
This site is from the White House. With an introduction from President Bill Clinton and biographies that include each president's inaugural address, this site is excellent. Get information on White House history, art in the White House, first ladies, first families, and much more.

POTUS—Presidents of the United States
http://www.ipl.org/ref/POTUS/
In this resource you will find background information, election results, cabinet members, presidency highlights, and some odd facts on each of the presidents. Links to biographies, historical documents, audio and video files, and other presidential sites are also included to enrich this site.

These sites are subject to change. Go to your favorite search engine and type in United States presidents for more sites.

Pass It On

History enthusiasts: educate readers around the country by passing on information you've learned about presidents or other important people who've changed history. Share your little-known facts and interesting stories. We want to hear from you!

To get posted on the ABDO Publishing Company Web site, email us at:
history@abdopub.com
Visit the ABDO Publishing Company Web site at www.abdopub.com

Index